C000001111

Rowley

ANTHONY H. PAGE

SUTTON PUBLISHING

Sutton Publishing Limited
Phoenix Mill · Thrupp · Stroud
Gloucestershire · GL5 2BU

First published 2001

Copyright © Anthony H. Page, 2001

Title page photograph: The third Parish
Church of St Giles, 1920. (*Author's
Collection*)

British Library Cataloguing in Publication Data
A catalogue record for this book is available from the
British Library.

ISBN 0-7509-2764 X

Typeset in 10.5/13.5 Photina.
Typesetting and origination by
Sutton Publishing Limited.
Printed and bound in England by
J.H. Haynes & Co. Ltd, Sparkford.

THE BLACK COUNTRY SOCIETY

This voluntary society, affiliated to the Civic Trust, was founded in 1967 as a reaction to the trend of the late 1950s and early 1960s to amalgamate everything into large units and in the Midlands to sweep away the area's industrial heritage in the process.

The general aim of the Society is to create interest in the past, present and future of the Black Country, and early on it campaigned for the establishment of an industrial museum. In 1975 the Black Country Living Museum was started by Dudley Borough Council on 26 acres of totally derelict land adjoining the grounds of Dudley Castle. This has developed into an award-winning museum which attracts over 250,000 visitors annually.

In 1998 the Museum Board secured a lottery grant of nearly £3 million towards the £4.5 million cost of building a state-of-the-art interpretation centre. Known as the Rolfe Street Baths Project as it incorporated that Smethwick building which was transferred to the museum site, it was officially opened on 18 May 2001. It includes two fine exhibition halls, administration and storage rooms and retains the original Victorian building's façade. The museum's already wide range of attractions is likely soon to be increased in the field of transport with the acquisition of two major collections of vehicles.

At the Black Country Living Museum there is a boat dock fully equipped to restore narrowboats of wood and iron and different vessels can be seen on the dock throughout the year. From behind the Bottle and Glass Inn visitors can travel on a canal boat into Dudley Canal Tunnel, a memorable journey to see spectacular limestone caverns and the fascinating Castle Mill Basin.

There are 2,650 members of the Black Country Society and all receive the quarterly magazine *The Blackcountryman*, of which 136 issues have been published since its founding in 1967. In the whole collection there are some 2,000 authoritative articles on all aspects of the Black Country by historians, teachers, researchers, students, subject experts and ordinary folk with an extraordinary story to tell. The whole constitutes a unique resource about the area and is a mine of information for students and researchers who frequently refer to it. Many schools and libraries are subscribers. Over 3,300 copies of the magazine are printed each quarter. It is non-commercial, and contributors do not receive payment for their articles.

PO Box 71 · Kingswinford · West Midlands DY6 9YN

CONTENTS

The coat of arms of Rowley Regis. The faces of the lions are in gold on a red field, and represent the lions of England; they are flanking a leg indicating the connection with the Haden family, whose ancestral home was Haden Hill Hall. The pale is ermine, the same as the bend in Lord Dudley's arms. The family of Somery bore 'Or two lions passant azure', and the blue lion passant on the gold chief illustrates the connection with this family. The crest of the family of Sutton, Lords Dudley, bore 'Or a lion rampant double-queued vert', and is represented here by a similar demi lion in the crest. The arms of Halesowen Priory were 'Azure a chevron argent between three fleurs-de-lis or', and a similar fleur-de-lis is shown in the crest. The anchor in the crest is representative of one of the trades of the district while the miner and the smith shown as supporters are also symbols of local industry. (*By kind permission of Sandwell Metropolitan Borough Council*)

INTRODUCTION

'Rowley Regis is, in my belief, the Heart of the Black Country'. These words are taken from the book *The History of the Black Country* by J. Wilson-Jones ARHisS, FSC. Although many other towns and villages in the region would no doubt dispute the assertion, the inhabitants of Rowley, who hold on proudly to their history and traditions, would agree with the sentiment. One of the oldest settlements in the area, Rowley is set high on a series of hills, some 3 miles to the south-east of Dudley and about 7 miles from Birmingham. In 1851, William White wrote, 'The parish of Rowley Regis comprises the large but indifferently built village of Rowley, seated on the declivity of a lofty hill . . . and about 20 hamlets, which are occupied chiefly by nailers, chain-makers, and the miners, forgemen, etc., employed in the extensive coal and iron works here'. Traditionally it was in the county of Staffordshire, the most southerly parish of the county, where it remained until 1966, for a short time moving into Worcestershire as part of the County Borough of Warley, and then in 1974 into the newly formed county of the West Midlands on the formation of the Metropolitan Borough of Sandwell.

The name Rowley derives from the two Anglo-Saxon words 'rough' and 'lea', meaning a clearing in woodland, in which there were a few basic dwelling places. The community would have been centred around the location of the present parish church, because people tended to congregate on high ground for safety reasons, and it is likely that there would have been a place of worship, before the advent of Christianity. The early beginnings of the settlement remain a mystery, but evidence of Roman occupation was found, when, in 1794, in the remains of a wall constructed from the local stone, an earthenware vessel was discovered which contained 120 silver Roman coins bearing the heads of various emperors. In 1932 more coins and a medallion from the time of Hadrian were found in Hawes Lane. Following the Norman Conquest large parts of the surrounding area, including Rowley, were given to William Fitz Ansculf, who built the impressive castle at Dudley, and following his death it passed through various strands of the family, Paganel, de Somery, de Sutton and more recently Ward. The area was a royal manor, and local tradition has it that King John had a hunting lodge here, and this could be one reason why Rowley is not mentioned in the 'Domesday Book'. The name Regis was added in the early 1300s, when the manor reverted to the ownership of the Crown on the death of John de Somery, and for a time became known as 'King's Rowley' or 'Rowley of the King'.

There is no proof of when the first church was built, although it is plain that it has always been sited on or near the location of the present building at the peak of the hill, and local tradition puts the date as being in the reign of King John (between 1199 and 1216). The parish registers are among the earliest known in the country, the first entry being the christening of Thomas, son of Richard Lyddiate, on 20 January 1539. The church, as far as can be ascertained, has always been dedicated to St Giles, who was the saint of the woodlands, reflecting the nature of the countryside around the hill. Although being some 8 miles apart, it was originally a chapel of ease, associated with St Leonard's, Clent (St Leonard again being a woodland saint), before becoming a parish in its own right in 1855.

One of the main dwelling places was Rowley Hall, situated close to the church, which was not completely demolished until the 1970s and found notoriety as a hiding place for two of the fleeing conspirators involved in the Gunpowder Plot, Robert Winter and Stephen Lyttleton, in late 1605. The Hall then passed through the hands of many of the major families who feature in the story of Rowley Regis. Perhaps the greatest change in the history and growth of Rowley came with the development of the coalfield, and the reliance on coal made by the industrial changes. The Earls of Dudley had been mining for centuries and had also been supplying iron nails to the Crown. In the early nineteenth century there were a total of thirty-one collieries in Rowley, most of which were in operation until the 1920s.

The quality of the rock was already widely known, and again there was a massive increase in the quarrying of the Rowley Rag, which was used throughout the region as the basis for the roads before the advent of tarmacadam. Most of the major highways in the developing city of Birmingham were made of crushed Rowley Rag, perhaps laid by Rowley roadmen. It was a time of living hard and taking what few pleasures there were, as and when it was possible. At one stage in the immediate area of the church there were upward of a dozen public ale houses, frequented by the home-going miners and quarrymen. The women and children were also pressed into service, with home-based nail shops being common, and Rowley was also a centre for the production of a now almost obsolete musical instrument, the jew's (or jaw's) harp.

There have been many notable personalities in the history of Rowley, some of whom will be found later in this book. It is highly probable that Lady Godiva had lands in the area and would have visited them. When Queen Elizabeth I travelled from Halesowen to Dudley in 1657 she passed through the village. Charles Darwin is believed to have spent time here when writing his *The Origin of Species*. The development of nearby Blackheath, the increase in educational facilities and the replacement of housing stock have all changed the Rowley of old, but the character remains in the people who populate the area.

1

The Local Scene

With a little imagination, this spectacular view of the Hailstone Quarry, taken in the mid-1950s, could be mistaken for a scene in the Italian Dolomites. At this time the Turners Hill road between the two quarries was still open for traffic. The Clent Hills can be seen on the horizon. (*Irene Harrold*)

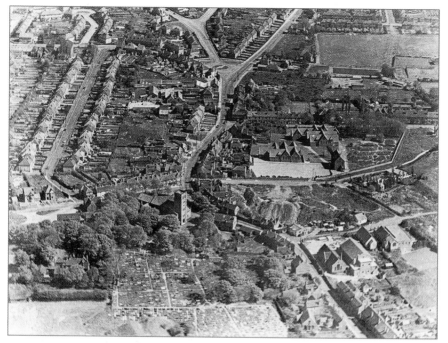

An aerial view of Rowley village, 1955. The parish church stands to the left of centre, with its extensive graveyard. Opposite is the small quarry with the school between Curral Road and Siviters Lane. The old cottages stand to each side of Church Road and the hill of Rowley village leads down to the traffic island at Bell End. (*Black Country Living Museum*)

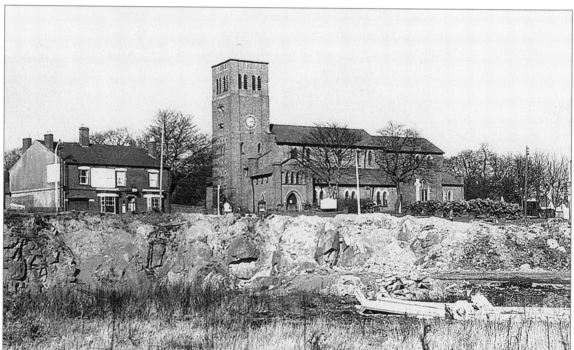

St Giles' Parish Church, viewed from Curral Road, February 1961. Note that The Ward Arms pub is still in use. The quarry in the foreground was originally about 100 ft deep, but at this time is being filled with hardcore in preparation for landscaping. Between the church and quarry once stood a row of cottages and opposite the pub was the wooden bungalow of Mr Albert Westwood (a shoemaker by trade, who later served as Mayor of Rowley Regis). These buildings were demolished in the 1950s. (*Derek Crump*)

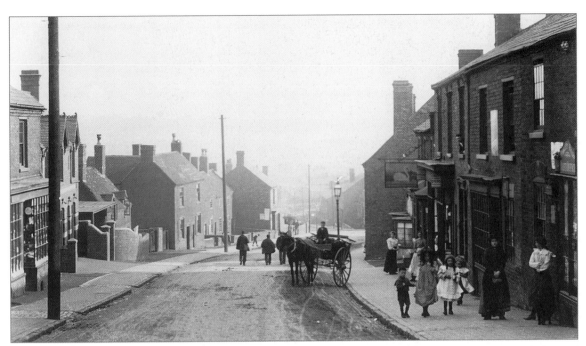

This postcard, dated 1906, shows the view from the church down Rowley village towards Blackheath, The Swan public house being visible on the right-hand side. (*Ken Rock Collection*)

A somewhat later view, probably in the mid-1920s, looking in the opposite direction. The typical Black Country cottages with their front door steps, which were a common sight at the time, mark the left-hand side of the picture. (*Ken Rock Collection*)

Church Road, *c*. 1910. The wall of the parish church is on the left, and the cottages and shops that remained until the 1950s are seen on the right. (*Author's Collection*)

The old St Giles' Vicarage, in Hanover Road, viewed from the churchyard, February 1961. (*Derek Crump*)

Another view of the village, with the third church, which occupied the site between 1904 and 1913, on the crest of the hill. (*Ken Rock Collection*)

A postcard of Siviters Lane, sent in 1924 to Mrs Wood in Chelmsford, Essex, explaining that this was the new family home and that the surroundings were very pleasant, although most of the household had been ill with flu. The school buildings are just visible on the left-hand side of the picture. (*Ken Rock Collection*)

Siviters Lane looking towards the top of Ross, mid-1930s. (*Ken Rock Collection*)

Overlooking the fields, the parish church can be seen on the horizon in this postcard of Siviters Lane taken from outside The Hollies at the top of Ross, *c.* 1920. (*Ken Rock Collection*)

The view from the junction of Bell End and Rowley village, May 1973. The shops on the left-hand side are the butcher's, and the general store of Jack and Gladys Troman. Britannia Road is on the right of the picture. (*CHAS*)

The old cottages on the corner of Bell End were replaced in the 1960s by a small development of flats, and from the bedroom of no. 12 there is a good view towards Blackheath, with The Britannia public house and electrical retailer's, in the old Co-op building, on the right. On a clear day the hills of Clent and Frankley can be seen on the horizon. (*Irene Harrold*)

Highbury, 33 Siviters Lane, the home of the Eley family from the mid-1930s until it was demolished in 1969 to make way for Siviters Close. Joseph and Sarah Eley started the butcher's and draper's shops in High Street, Blackheath. Of their five daughters, two were still living there in 1969: Ellen ('Nellie') Perry and Eileen Bryant, with husband Reg and daughters Gillian and Rosalynne. Reg's Ford Anglia is parked outside. (*Reg Bryant*)

One of the main employers in the area was T.W. Lench, manufacturers of nuts and bolts, and they took a pride in the welfare of the employees. Close to the factory was the recreation ground and park that included this pool. On reverse of this postcard is written 'This is our lake. It would be alright to take a nice girl a day's boating on here. How would you like to come?' To preserve anonymity there are no names given! (*Ken Rock Collection*)

One of the smaller quarries was given the name Rowley Hall, because it was owned by and situated in close proximity to the building of that name. The Hall had a chequered history from the time of its building in the late sixteenth century until the final demolition in 1970 (following a period of vandalism and decay). In 1605 it was owned by Christopher White, a relative of Stephen Lyttleton of Holbeache House, Kingswinford, who was deeply implicated in the Gunpowder Plot. It is thought that some of the conspirators, fleeing justice, were sheltered in the cellars of Rowley Hall before making their escape. The Hall, positioned at the summit of the hill, was subsequently owned by several families, including that of 'Squire Beet' in the nineteenth century (whose name gives rise to Beet Street, Blackheath), Frederick North who opened Rowley Hall Colliery in about 1870 and finally Jack Noott. (*CHAS*)

Pictures of Rowley Hall seem to be hard to find, but this was the main doorway taken just before demolition. (*Colin Beet*)

A watercolour impression of Rowley Mill as it would have looked in about 1802, with Allsop's Hill in background. Later a similar mill was to be found in the area called Windmill End. (*Horace Wilson*)

This row of cottages are awaiting demolition in 1971. They were known as Club Buildings and were situated at right angles to Hawes Lane, which can be seen in the background. (*CHAS*)

This house was the home of the quarry manager and was to be found opposite the Conservative Club in Hawes Lane. It was built in the early part of the nineteenth century and was demolished for a proposed road-widening and straightening scheme, which never happened. It was called Prospect House after the name of the quarry, which was later incorporated into Allsop's Quarry. (*David Westwood*)

This row of cottages was in Hawes Lane, between the Conservative Club and the old Church of England school, and is seen here on 30 August 1971. (*CHAS*)

Another earlier view of Hawes Lane looking in the direction of Turners Hill, 1907. (*Horace Wilson*)

The remains of the site of the disused reservoir situated off Bell End and Newhall Road, November 1968. It first held water in 1877 but although originally constructed to contain 3 million gallons, it was never totally filled. After damage and cracking, probably caused by the proximity of mining operations, it was finally abandoned in 1924. This photograph was taken just prior to the area being redeveloped into Cambourne Road and Reservoir Road. (*CHAS*)

Mary Ann Hadley with her son Arthur outside their cottage in Bell End, at the top of Mincing Lane, *c.* 1920. The tramway carrying coal from the pits to the canal wharf used to travel at the rear of these premises, and it was commonplace for the youngsters of the area to keep their families supplied with winter fuel by picking lumps of coal from the trams and throwing them over the garden walls. (*Alfred Hadley*)

A few doors away towards the junction with the village, Pauline Harrold is pictured on the driveway of her home at 27 Bell End. Note that at the time, *c.* 1930, there is open space at the rear as the housing in Park Avenue has not yet been built. (*Margaret Sheward*)

A row of cottages in the lower part of Rowley village, just below the post office, 1961. The same families tended to occupy the premises from generation to generation, the Aldridge household at no. 38; the Woodalls at no. 39; the Bennetts at no. 40. (*Ray Parkes*)

Brickhouse Farm was situated between the Rowley Hills and Old Hill. In this picture, taken from Moor Lane in 1956, the last few cows are grazing on the land, which was to become the playing fields of the grammar school. The first few houses of the large council estate that eventually bore the name of the farm are just visible. (*Irene Harrold*)

Some of the first houses on the Brickhouse Farm estate await completion, mid-1950s. (*Margaret Sheward*)

Portway Hall was erected in 1671 and originally belonged to the Johnson family, who were yeomen farmers. It started life as a half-timbered house, but was converted and extended in the early part of the nineteenth century into the structure seen here. It eventually passed into the hands of the Pardoe family (see p. 114). (*Ken Rock Collection*)

These ornamental tiles formed part of the porchway of Portway Hall, pictured shortly before the building was demolished in 1979. (*CHAS*)

One of the hamlets belonging to Rowley was Oakham, situated at the top of Turners Hill, seen here in about 1910. This is the view looking towards Dudley. The early road from the outskirts of Birmingham to Dudley followed the track known as Portway, and would have passed through this area. (*Mabel Smith*)

The farmhouse at Warrens Hall Farm, situated on the Oakham Road, *c.* 1960. It was later developed into riding stables and then was converted to a residential nursing home. (*Mabel Smith*)

The pool at Warrens Hall Farm in the winter of 1988. It was filled in a few years later to prepare for a small housing development. It is believed that there was a well close by, but in the name of progress that too has probably disappeared. (*Mabel Smith*)

Oakham Road, at the junction with Darby's Hill Road, showing the cottage of George Smith, *c.* 1928. Smith achieved notoriety as 'The Dudley Hangman', assisting in and later performing many executions. Also seen are the Hangman's Tree, immortalised by a public house bearing the same name, with Wellfield House in the background. (*CHAS*)

Dog Lane was just on the extreme edge of the parish of Rowley Regis before it became Netherton, and in the shadow of the embankment of the Great Western Railway line lay the small farm belonging to Solomon Danks, seen here in the late nineteenth century. A brook ran through the property and it was therefore the ideal place to grow watercress, and the extensive beds are seen in the foreground, while Solomon and members of the family pose behind them. (*Norah Smith*)

Following a hard day's work, many a long evening would be spent gathered around the hearth, such as this typical example from an old Rowley cottage which dates from 1658. As can be seen, the fireplace was multi-purpose, serving not only to heat the room, but also to cook the food, with the pots and kettles in constant use. (*Author's Collection*)

Britannia Park, 1970. This area was, and still is, a peaceful green haven, and this view from the top end of the park shows the immaculate flower beds, looking over the nursery school and the greenhouses, towards Bell End, with the roof of the Baptist chapel dominating the skyline and Oldbury on the horizon. (*Vera Guest*)

Rowley did not escape damage during the Second World War, with several properties being destroyed by German bombs, and the aftermath of one such raid resulted in the total demolition of this cottage. (*Author's Collection*)

The Barley Mow inn, near the quarry at Darby's Hill, *c.* 1907. (*Horace Wilson*)

Situated in close proximity to the location above, this is City Road, Oakham, approximately thirty years later, from near The Barley Mow. The former name of the road was Gipsy Lane. The petrol pump at this time was dispensing 'Pratt's Gasoline'. (*CHAS*)

The large outcrop of rock seen in this engraving by W.W. Baker, published in 1845, was given the name 'Rowley Hailstone', and was thought at one time to be indestructible. From the summit of the rock there were unsurpassed views over the whole region, but it had been removed by the summer of 1879, with festivities held to celebrate the event. Frederick Wright was killed in February 1879 in the process of uprooting the rock, and one of the last men to bore shot holes, Benjamin Bate, was killed in December 1879. After the removal of the rock a tramway incline was made in 1880, connecting the quarry to the canal at Windmill End. (*Horace Wilson*)

The large hole that is the result of many years of quarrying of Rowley Rag in the Hailstone and other quarries, which over time have merged into one. The large earth-moving equipment, lorries and personnel are dwarfed in this picture, which was taken in the late 1960s. (*David Westwood*)

Portway Hill still retains its rural origins, which are seen in this photograph taken before road-widening in the 1960s turned it into the busy thoroughfare of today. (*Arthur Hadley*)

An excursion steam train enters Rowley Regis station in the 1960s, bringing back memories of a bygone age. (*Eric Parkes*)

A postcard, dated 1913, sent by a lad to his mother in Essex, with the message 'this is the view of where I shall be working'. The mine was known as Perry's Lake, or Knowle Colliery, and has a backdrop of Turners Hill. (*Ken Rock Collection*)

2

Schools

To celebrate the centenary of the foundation of the former Knowle Infants School in 1877, the descendants of the first pupils turned back the clock and dressed in Victorian clothes. Here we see Elizabeth Edmunds, aged six, Jason Cubberley and Emma Black, both aged five. (*Christine Young*)

The premises of Knowle Infants School, situated on Dudley Road, with the caretaker Mr Cooper looking over the walls, *c.* 1970. The school was demolished shortly afterwards to make way for the building of the special school, but construction is currently under way on this site to provide a new school for the twenty-first century. (*Gladys Troman*)

A class at Rowley Regis Church of England Infants School, which was situated in Hawes Lane opposite the parish church, 1915. (*Enid Hadley*)

The same school, showing teachers, prefects, captains and vice-captains, 1927. The teachers were Mr H. Hopcroft (headmaster), Mr B. Willetts, Miss Sheppey, Mrs Timmins and Miss G. Hodgetts; and the pupils seen here are John Beasley, Marjorie Page, Rachel Limbert, 'Curly' Dallow, Doris Devonport, Lily Rose, Alf Cole, Margaret Darby, Jim Beasley, Fred Horton, Bill Dowell and Arthur Southall. (*Jim Beasley*)

A class at Rowley Regis Church of England Infants School, 1928. A typical scene in a junior school class, with hard desks and inkwells, this could have been taken at any number of schools in the Black Country. (*Denise Macdonald*)

Rowley Regis Church of England Infants School football team of 1926/7, with the vicar Mr Cheverton. The player at the left of the front row was Fred Harrold, who later kept a grocer's shop and general stores in Bell End. (*Linda Harrold*)

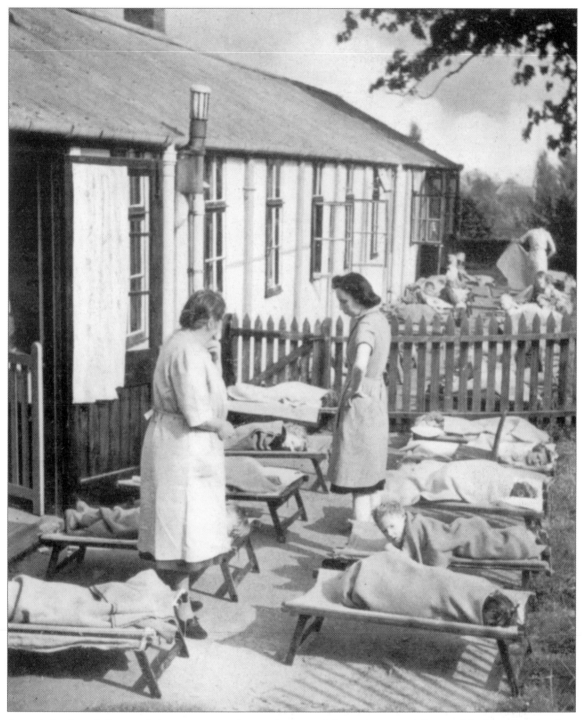

One of the first full-time day nurseries in the area operated from these pre-fabricated buildings situated in Britannia Park, seen here in about 1950. On a peaceful summer's day the children are taking their compulsory afternoon nap, watched over by the attendants. (*Margaret Sheward*)

Knowle Infants School, just prior to its demolition in 1975. It had not been used for the previous five years. (*Christine Young*)

In 1977, to celebrate the centenary of the founding of the Knowle Infants School, Springfield Infants, as it was then called, held a Black Country evening. Seen here (left to right) are: Mr Winston Homer, Councillor Dr Hiren Roy (Mayor of Sandwell), Councillor Syd Pemberton, Mrs Annie Bloom, Miss Nina Rogers (headmistress), Mrs Gladys Pemberton, Mr John Robinson, Mr Jim Jones and Miss Mavis Bostock. (*County Express*)

Miss Maud Westwood MA was born in Old Hill and educated at Halesowen Grammar School and Birmingham University. When she was appointed as headteacher of Rowley Regis Secondary School for Girls (popularly known as Siviters Lane) in 1947 she was one of the youngest women in the country to hold such a position. She was well respected by pupils and staff alike, and ensured that pupils received an all-round education. She retired in 1972, just prior to the amalgamation of the school with the boys school at Britannia Road. (*Maud Shaw*)

On 27 June 1952 a party of 320, including staff, governors, parents and girls, from Siviters Lane made a trip to London. After a tour of the capital by coach, taking in all of the major sites, the party was met in New Palace Yard by Mr Arthur Henderson QC, MP for a conducted tour around the Houses of Parliament, and members of the group are seen here on the terrace of the House of Commons. (*Maud Shaw*)

The school choir of Rowley Regis County Secondary School for Boys (Britannia Road), 1958. The teachers seen here are Mr Hickman, Mr Woodward and Mr Harris, and the pupils include David While, Terry Taylor, Alan Roberts, Alan Tranter, David Hackett, Billy Butler, Billy Bennett, Malcolm Tolley, Micky While, Billy Ross and Jimmy Hackett. (*David Hackett*)

From the same school the prefects are seen here with the headmaster Mr G.A. Willetts, 1946. The boys are, back row (left to right): M. Wilton, D. Cutler, R. Bowater, D. Taylor, F. Andrews, H. Taylor; front row: G. Worth, R. Faulkner, R. Stevens, M. Evans. (*Alan Atkinson*)

Pupils at the boys school are putting on a brave face on the school playing field dressed in their swimming gear, 1957. The school at Britannia Road was one of the few in the area to have its own indoor swimming pool, and so it is not surprising that they sponsored a large life-saving club. Mr G.A. Willetts with Wesley Potter (a Rowley boy on placement doing his teaching practice) to his left adopt a more dour appearance. (*David Hackett*)

ROWLEY REGIS URBAN DISTRICT

𝕰𝖉𝖚𝖈𝖆𝖙𝖎𝖔𝖓 𝕮𝖔𝖒𝖒𝖎𝖙𝖙𝖊𝖊.

OPENING OF
Rowley Regis Siviter's Lane Council School,
1st JULY, 1904.

PROGRAMME of PROCEEDINGS

1.—Opening of door at 3 o'clock p.m. and admission of guests invited.

2.—Assembly in the main hall of the mixed department.

3.—Prayer by the REV. A. F. DAUGLISH.

4.—National Anthem.   Solo by Mr. G. BROWN.
                                          Repeated by audience.

5.—Declaration by GEORGE GREEN, ESQ., J.P., Chairman of the Education Committee, that the School is open, and speech by him.

6.—Speech by E. W. COLT, ESQ., His Majesty's Inspector of Schools.

7.—Speech by SIR BENJAMIN HINGLEY, BART.

8.—Speech by G. B. HINGLEY, ESQ.

9.—Other speeches.

10.—Inspection of school-rooms and equipments.

> At the close of the speeches, the guests are desired to pass through and inspect the rooms and equipments, first in the building where they are assembled, then in the infants' department in the upper part of the playground, and afterwards through those for Handicraft and Laundry work. The Handicraft room is approached from the boys' playgronnd, and the Laundry room from the girls' playground, but both are in one building.

11.—Return to the Mixed Department for light refreshments.

Kindly bring this Programme to the Ceremony.

Accommodation for Gentlemen's Hats, &c., in boys' corridor, in charge of an attendant

Accommodation for Ladies' Cloaks, &c,, in girls' corridor, in charge of an attendant

Rowley Regis Siviters Lane Council School was officially opened on 1 July 1904, and this was the cover of the 'Programme of Proceedings'. The accompanying notes state that the school accommodates 310 children for elementary daily school work, and on the opening morning 277 pupils were present. In order for the ceremony to take place they were given a half-day holiday in the afternoon. The headmaster of the mixed department was Mr A.E. Bloomer, assisted by teachers from Birmingham Road School. Headmistress of the infants department was Miss E. Caddick, also helped by staff from Birmingham Road and Rowley Regis National Infants School. (*Maud Shaw*)

(*Opposite bottom*): Miss Westwood was responsible for writing many Nativity plays for the girls to perform, but also encouraged other members of staff to create and produce dramatic and musical events. Here we see some of the cast of a production by Mr A. Wildman of his own 'Pageant of Rowley Regis', which traced the history of the village from earliest time to the then present day. The climax was the appearance, in full robes, of the Mayor Councillor Albert Westwood, himself an old boy of the school. (*Maud Shaw*)

The practical room at Siviters Lane, where the girls were instructed in the domestic arts, 1931. The girls present include: Gladys Taylor, Doris Mucklow, Edith Hobbs, Irene Green, Phyllis Smith, Leila Dunn, Rachel Limbert, Ivy Goodwin, ? Thompson, Rose Woodhouse, Doris Wilton, Muriel Billingham, Doris Willetts, ? Brown, Miriam Whale, Winnie Yates, ? Haden, Margaret Bettinson, Iris Parsons, Gladys Bennett, Margaret Hall, Irene Lee, ? Robinson, Emily Whitehouse, Millicent Sleigh, Irene Hadley, Beatrice Bishop, Ivy Dyas, Elsie Cole, Cissie Hall, Mary Dyas, ? Darby, ? Bridgewater, Rose Cutler. (*Minnie Johnson*)

The Nativity play of 1952, with some of the cast surrounding Miss Westwood. (*Mary Cutler*)

The Siviters Lane school choir in the plantation, October 1951. When the school was opened in 1904, each pupil planted a sapling, which over the years grew into this secluded area, well loved by the scholars and local residents alike. (*Mary Cutler*)

The staff of Knowle Infants School, 1967. They are, back row (left to right): Yvonne Hackett, Mrs Tromans (school secretary), Dorothy Hughes; front row: Eileen Jones, Miss M.E. Tubb (headmistress), Jean Grainger and Joan Gardner. (*Christine Young*)

Oakham Primary School staff, 1971/2. Standing (left to right): Rita West, Carol Shakespeare, Jean Boulton, Jenny Eden, Pat Grainger, Tim O'Mara, Wendy Nichol, Edna Carter, Bryan Jones, Mrs Gray, Mrs Worton; seated: Cynthia Emson, Mrs Schofield, Mrs Reed, David Eades (deputy head), Mr R.D. Worton (headmaster), Wendy Williams and Philip Jones. (*David Eades*)

The girls at Siviters Lane school formed an orchestra, seen here in 1971, which was directed at this time by Mr W.E. Hancox. In addition to performing within the school, at speech days and the like, they also raised a lot of money for local charities by giving recitals and concerts. (*Maud Shaw*)

The class of 1929 at Siviters Lane Infants School. Back row (left to right): Frank Ingram, Albert Darby, Frank Hadley, Billy Goode, Leslie Baker, Leonard Griffiths, John Adams, Arthur Swift; centre row: Fred Cole, Wesley Adams, Bob Marshall, Alf Adams, Stan Willetts, Leonard Hanson, Derek Williams, Billy Andrews, Jack Shaw; front row: Doug Partridge, Joe Bridgewater, Eric Hill, John Batsford, Ray Bridgewater, Arthur Parkes, Jack Shakespeare. (*Ray Bridgewater*)

Mr George T. Lloyd JP, MA, the headmaster of Rowley Regis Grammar School, who took up his duties in January 1948, having previously been senior English master at the County High School, Bromsgrove. The school was then situated in Wright's Lane, Old Hill, and he was responsible for ensuring the move to the new premises in Hawes Lane was accomplished as efficiently as possible. He was highly regarded inside and outside the school, and for many years was a Methodist local preacher of some note. (*Malcolm Warby*)

The new buildings that made up Rowley Regis Grammar School, in Hawes Lane, 1962. Occupying an elevated site of 27 acres, which was originally a mixture of pastureland, quarry faces and spoil heaps, it was a marked improvement on the old crowded premises in Wright's Lane. It was designed to house a total of 1,000 pupils, and at the time of opening there were 450. It began to be used in part on 1 March 1962, and was fully operational by October of that year. (*Malcolm Warby*)

The presentation of a new minibus at Oakham Primary School, January 1973. The school was the first primary school in the County Borough of Warley to own such a vehicle; the cost of the bus and of erecting a garage to house it on school grounds was raised by the efforts of children, parents and staff. Standing near the bus are Mr R.D. Worton (headteacher), Mr D.L. Eades (deputy head), Mrs Mullett (parent) and Councillor W. Walker (chairman of the school managers). (County Express)

A class of pupils from Rowley Hall Primary School visit the nearby quarry, and pose for the camera in their hard hats, 1972. (*Carol Hurley*)

A very old school photograph, thought to date from about 1890. The slate tells us it is class 2, and possibly says Rowley Infants, but further details are not known. (*Joan Gardner*)

Girls from Siviters Lane go 'native' during a school trip to Belgium and Holland in the early 1960s. (*Maud Shaw*)

The school hall was always packed when it was the annual speech day at Siviters Lane school, and here we see the girls and invited guests in 1958. (County Express)

For the children of the Black Country, a trip into the countryside was always a welcome adventure, especially in the years immediately after the Second World War, and from the happy looks on the faces of these girls from Siviters Lane, they are obviously enjoying being under canvas at the Beaudesert camp, Cannock, *c.* 1948. (*Mary Cutler*)

3

Churches & Chapels

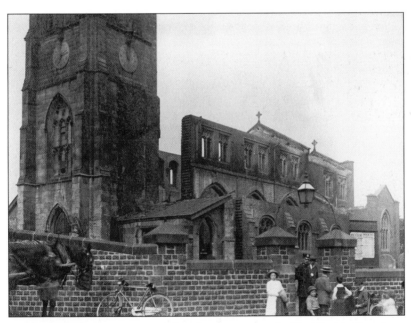

The local policeman stands guard at the entrance to St Giles' Parish Church, as people gather to survey the damage caused by the devastating fire that occurred on the night of 18 June 1913. The foundation stone for this building was laid on 27 June 1904, and it was opened later in that year. The 1858 tower of the previous church remained standing until April 1915, when it was declared unsafe and taken down to within 6 ft of the ground. (*Malcolm Warby*)

It is widely believed that the first church of St Giles was positioned very close to where the present building stands, and dated from about 1200. It stood until 1840 when it was demolished and rebuilt, and from this F. Jones' lithograph of the second church, published by Day & Sons, it was an ornate structure with an extended tower. (*CHAS*)

This unusual view of the third church on the site shows a small gathering watching a monumental mason at work in the churchyard. The memorial is dedicated to Joseph Walters, who died on 1 January 1894, his wife Phoebe, who died on 1 January 1911, and their son Joseph, who died aged two years and six months on 15 December 1878. The family address was Rowley village. (*Frances Dolphin*)

The exterior of the third church of St Giles, photographed in 1907, some two years after it was completed. It included the tower of the previous building, which had been modified in 1858, and had a comparatively short life, being destroyed in 1913. (*Horace Wilson*)

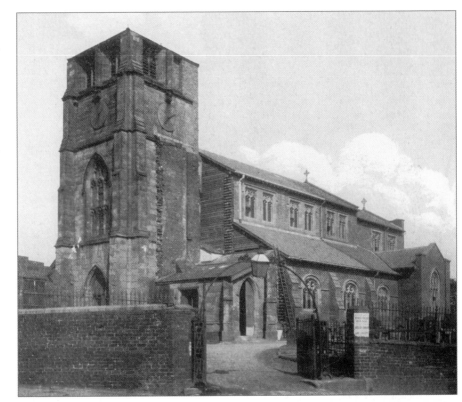

The chancel of the third church. (*Ken Rock Collection*)

Local stories abound about the fire that destroyed the third parish church on the night of 18 June 1913. On the previous evening several well-dressed ladies wearing large hats were seen in the vicinity, giving rise to the possibility of action by the suffragettes. The steel workers at Coombes Wood were striking at the time, and they too have been blamed, as have a group of Irish labourers seen in the area. The church was heated by paraffin heaters and there had been a meeting held during the evening, so it is likely that it was a tragic accident, but we shall probably never know! (*Ken Rock Collection*)

Worship continues in the shell of the burnt-out church, led by the Revd Mr Cheverton. For a period, however, parish duties were carried out from the associated buildings on the opposite side of Hawes Lane. (*Malcolm Warby*)

The fourth, and present, parish church was dedicated in 1923, on the feast of St Michael and All Angels (Saturday, 29 September), by the Lord Bishop of Birmingham. This in itself gave rise to some consternation, as the vicar wished to name the new church in honour of St Michael, but following massive public opposition accepted that the tradition of St Giles should continue. It is noted that at the dedication the local band of bell-ringers was able 'to ring a touch of Grandsire Triples'. (*Malcolm Warby*)

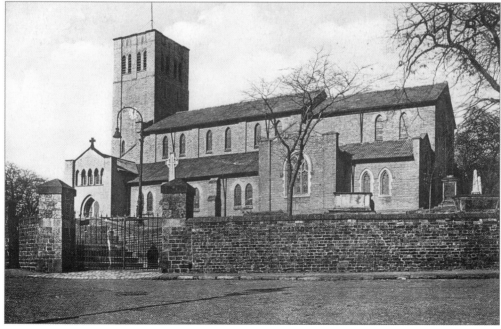

The interior of the fourth church shortly after opening, equipped with gas lighting. (*Malcolm Warby*)

A familiar sight in and around St Giles' Parish Church was Jethro Sidaway. He was unique in that he lived to see all four of the churches. He was baptised in the first church on 24 November 1839 by the Revd George Barrs and was present at the dedication of the fourth church in 1923. (*Author's Collection*)

The Rowley Regis village war memorial was unveiled and dedicated to the memory of those who gave their lives in the First World War on Saturday, 4 September 1920. The guard of honour was provided by the Harborne Training School Cadet Corps and the cross was unveiled by Brigadier General W.R. Ludlow CB, who also gave the address. The dedication was made by the Venerable Archdeacon C.E. Hopton, and memorial services were held in the ruins of the church on the following day. (*Enid Hadley*)

Associated with St Giles' Parish Church were the Rowley Regis Adult Education Class, seen here in 1913. John Parkes is fourth from left on the second row from front. (*Ray Parkes*)

Local Scouts and Guides entering St Giles' Parish Church for a parade service, 1961. (*Malcolm Warby*)

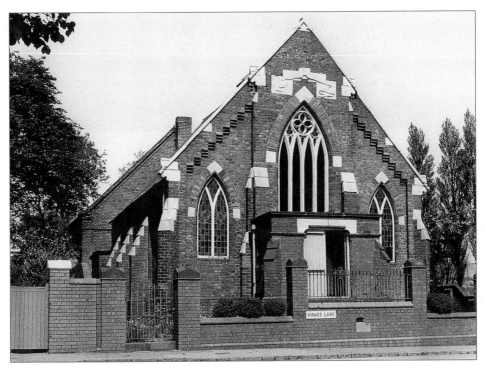

Hawes Lane Methodist Church and Sunday School, in use from 1862 to 1899, when the new schoolroom was built at the rear. It was renovated in 1927 when a new front porch was added and the front wall built. It was demolished in 1973 to make way for the planned road-widening. (*CHAS*)

A rare photograph of the interior of Hawes Lane Methodist Church, dating from about the beginning of the twentieth century. The high central pulpit is lit by the original gas lamps. The last service was held on 4 October 1970. (*CHAS*)

In this photograph of the Sunday School anniversary celebrations of about 1950 that took place at Hawes Lane Methodist Church there are seven children from the Westwood family. In total there were fourteen children, and their father Albert became Mayor of Rowley Regis. Among those pictured are: Ann Huyton, Margaret Clayton, Jean Gilbert, Janet Williams, Alice Horton, Ruby Whittall, Freda Westwood, Barry Nock, Tony Murray, June Woodhall, Pat Wood, Ann Taylor, Mabel Hill, Joan Yates, Dorothy Westwood, Eunice Willmott, Dennis Westwood, Maurice Brown, Clive Westwood, May Yates, Jill Aldridge, Doreen Rann, Mary Bennett, June Drew, Sheila Murray, Maureen Murray, June Nock, Brenda Dyas, June Souter, Howard Westwood, Georgina Chater, Kathleen Westwood, Pat Northall, Pam Northall, Anna Cooper, Beryl Jennings and Janet Westwood. (*Jill Wroe*)

The Sunday School scholars and teachers of the Endowed School Mission, Rowley village, pose for the camera in 1953. (*Anita Whitehouse*)

One of the smaller churches in the region is the Church in the Garden, situated in Ross. It was started by Walter Darby and was used as a depot for the worldwide distribution of tracts and leaflets on behalf of 'The Homeland Missionary Society'. Back row (left to right): Albert Williams, Ron Shaw, Albert Homer, Ben Hill, Ernie Hodgetts, Lawson Darby; front row: James Parkes, Walter Darby, Pastor Jeffries, Joe Shepherd and Brian Homer. (*Martin Pearson*)

The Church in the Garden was literally that, meetings taking place in the shed in the back garden of Walter Darby's home. Despite modifications over the years, the building became unfit for use, and in October 1991, led by Walter's grandson Martin, a new structure was built and remains in use today. Here the contrast between the old and the new can be clearly seen. (*Martin Pearson*)

George Aldridge (on the steps of the caravan) was born in Rowley village in 1876, and lived there for all of his eighty-six years. He became a miner from the age of thirteen, but when he was twenty-five he read an article about a blind preacher called Christmas Evans, and as a result George ventured into a prayer meeting at Hawes Lane Methodist Church, something he had never done before. He was converted and became a local preacher, and at the age of thirty

was offered a position of evangelist by the West Midlands Federation, and from that day he travelled in this caravan all over the West Midlands preaching the gospel. Unfortunately, after ten years his health deteriorated, and he had to give up touring. He set up, firstly, as a grocer and then the sub-post master in the village. He preached his last sermon at the Endowed Mission Hall, opposite the post office, when he was over eighty years of age. (*Mavis Bates*)

The origins of Methodism in the area then called The Knowle, later to become Springfield, began back in 1861, when preachers from Darby End conducted open-air services on the ground at the top of what is now Springfield Lane. It was decided to build a permanent church, and land was purchased in 1868, the church opening the following year. The schoolroom was added later, in 1898, and this was the view at the turn of the nineteenth century. (*Kenneth Biggs*)

The Girls Life Brigade of Knowle Methodist Church, with the company chaplain the Revd H. Highfield, 4 July 1936. Those identified are: Beatrice Dunn (left of flag), Norah Dunn (right of flag) and John (Jack) Biggs in Scout uniform on the left-hand side. (*Kenneth Biggs*)

The 1898 schoolroom at Knowle was much affected by subsidence, and was partially demolished, but by 1950 had become a public liability. Permission was obtained to replace it and on 23 August 1952 it was closed.

Mr Ernest Price, the former superintendent of the Sunday School, is seen here ceremonially knocking out the first brick. (*Kenneth Biggs*)

Members of Knowle Methodist Church meet outside the old schoolroom on 23 August 1952. This was just before its demolition and the construction of new premises, which were to cost £8,000, a considerable sum at the time. (*Kenneth Biggs*)

Joseph Parkes was born in Hackett Street, Blackheath, in about 1820, and in adult life was a nail-maker by trade. His great love, however, was the composition of hymn music. He often left his nail block to write down a tune, and as a consequence he and his family went hungry because he was not earning a living. Most of his tunes including those called 'Carr's Lane', 'Bower Street', 'Eastern Star' and 'Diadem' are no longer in use, but the one dedicated to his home area 'Rowley Regis' is still in popular use around the West Midlands, and has been taken as far as Dorset, Devon and Walthamstow by Black Country emigrants. It is sung to the Epiphany hymn of Joseph Heber 'Brightest and Best of the Sons of the Morning'. (*Author's Collection*)

(*Opposite bottom*): Alfred Dye was born in Norfolk in 1851, and was called to be pastor at Bell End in 1888, a position he retained for over thirty-five years. He was a well-known preacher throughout the country, as well as being a poet and hymn-writer. The family are seen here in 1912 in the garden of the manse (left to right): Rachel Mary, Ruth Esther, Mercy Alice, Alfred Dye, Alfred Muskett, Mrs Elizabeth Dye, Leah Elizabeth and Abigail May. (*Evelyn Rose*)

The Strict Baptists had founded a chapel in Bell End at the beginning of the nineteenth century, but due to doctrinal difficulties it weakened until it closed down for a short time. In 1828 the premises were purchased by Daniel Matthews and Betty Mountford, who remained loyal until her death and was grateful to the way God had provided for her, which inspired them to rename the chapel 'Providence'. Matthews, a rivet-maker, was instrumental in raising funds for a new chapel, opened in 1876, free of debt, seen here in the early 1900s with the adjoining manse. (*Gladys Troman*)

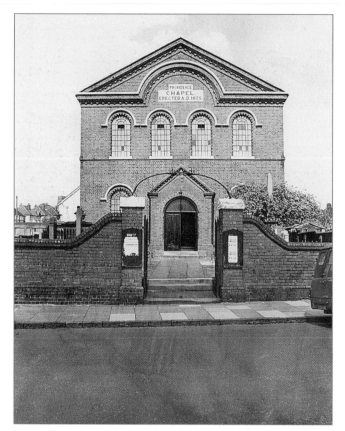

Providence Strict and Particular
Baptist Chapel, Bell End,
20 May 1973. (*CHAS*)

Pastor Tim Martin moved from
Providence Chapel in December
1984, and members of the
church held a tea and
presented him and his wife
with gifts to celebrate their
service to the church. (*Gladys
Troman*)

Standing between the Methodist church in Hawes Lane and the parish church was the Ebenezer Strict and Particular Baptist Chapel, known locally as Ruston's Chapel. For whatever reason, Joseph Ruston and his family became disaffected with the way things were going at Providence and after meeting for a short time in Mr Ruston's home, they built Ebenezer. It was opened for worship on Christmas Day 1897, closed in September 1979 and demolished in August 1981. (*David Westwood*)

A plaque on the wall of the Ebenezer Chapel dedicated to Joseph Ruston and reading 'This place was raised by the church and hearers of Joseph Ruston, 1897.' One of the local oral traditions is that it was the introduction of an organ into Bell End that caused the split, and it is true that for many years the singing at Ebenezer was unaccompanied, being pitched by the leader with a tuning fork. (*David Westwood*)

The Ladies Fellowship Class at the Endowed School Mission, *c.* 1980. Among those pictured are: Kathleen Neale, Sheila Hudson, Muriel Tromans, Wendy Barnsley, Maureen Baggott, Josie Smith, Carol Nock, Pauline Johnson, Mrs C.B. Adams, Flo Davies, Daphne Allen, Jill Rowe, Iris Hadley, Brenda Johnson, Mrs Potter, Winnie Johnson and Minnie Johnson. (*Jill Rowe*)

The members of the Rowley Regis Endowed School pose outside their current building, 1987. The adults include: Iris Deeley, Tony Adams, Paul Adams, Ben Johnson, Cheryl Jones, Ron Walker, Alan Johnson and Mary Adams. (*Arthur Hadley*)

Darby's Hill Mission and Sunday
School at the top of Portway Hill, at
the junction with the cutting
through the quarries in Turners Hill,
18 May 1969. (*CHAS*)

The Sunday School treat at Darby's
Hill Mission, *c.* 1955. The lady in the
centre is Evelyn Cole, with the
church secretary Arthur Willis on
the extreme right-hand side. (*Arthur
Hadley*)

The Christmas party at Darby's Hill Mission, 1958. Father Christmas was Arthur Hadley, and also seen are Brian Adams, Cecil Johnson, Audrey Johnson, John Hadley, Eileen Roberts and Iris Hadley. (*Arthur Hadley*)

Members of Knowle Methodist Church Girls Life Brigade, in costume and uniform at what was possibly a missionary event, *c.* 1935. Beatrice Biggs (née Dunn) is on the left-hand side, Norah Dunn (later Flavell) at centre back and Edie Biggs on the right-hand side. (*Kenneth Biggs*)

The rambling group of Knowle United Methodist Church, as it then was, outside the church premises, 27 June 1914. (*Kenneth Biggs*)

The baptistry of the present St Giles' Parish Church, *c.* 1930. (*Malcolm Warby*)

The civic service of 1965, held at St Giles' Parish Church. At the head of the procession is the Mayor of Rowley Regis Urban District Council, Councillor Mrs Evelyn Matthews and her husband Ron, who are seen entering the west door of the church, flanked by members of organisations representing the life of the borough. (*Malcolm Warby*)

There are many large family vaults to be found in the churchyard of St Giles', this one belonging to the Beet family. John Beet, known as 'Squire Beet' (1774–1844) lived at Rowley Hall, and the grave is to his memory and other members of the family, including his daughter Elizabeth, who was the wife of the Very Revd W.A. Newman DD, Dean of Cape Town. (*Author*)

4

Work
& Leisure

Bell End Colliery, which was sited between Bell End and where the present-day Sandford Avenue stands, 1910. It was owned by H.S. Pitt & Company, which also worked the nearby Ramrod Colliery. (*Ken Rock Collection*)

A group of four gangers from the Bell End Colliery, including Frank Tromans (second from left), *c.* 1915. Frank lived with his sister and brother-in-law, Bill and Lily Grove, at 9 Bell End, which was at the other end of the lane from the pit and almost on the corner with Rowley village, before the houses were demolished in about 1985. (*Jean Bubb*)

Coal was first produced at Rowley Hall Colliery in about 1870, and the first proprietor was Frederick North, who lived with his family at Rowley Hall. It later passed into the hands of Walter Bassano, who was Chairman of the Board of Health of Rowley Regis. The workings were eventually discontinued in 1919, shortly after this photograph was taken. (*CHAS*)

Sir Henry Doulton (1820–97) from a
drawing by Frederick Sandys. Part of
the famous Potteries family, he
established, in 1848, a sanitary pipe
works in Rowley, in the road later to be
named after him. He visited the works
once a fortnight, usually arriving from
Birmingham by canal. He would spend
two days there, discussing business with
the managers and taking personal trips
round the works talking to those
employed. A number of women,
previously employed as nail- or chain-
makers came to work at the factory,
and on one visit Henry was appalled to
find them stripped to the waist, as they
had been used to working. After much
opposition he eventually had the
custom stopped, but declared in his
memoirs that the Rowley women had
always been a particular problem for
him. (*Horace Wilson*)

The main offices of Doulton & Company, in Doulton Road, in the late 1960s. The factory was
coming to the end of its production at this time. (*CHAS*)

An overview of the works yard at Doulton's, July 1969. (*CHAS*)

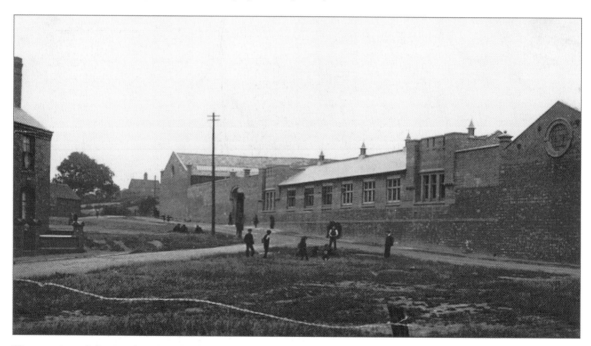

The exterior of the Excelsior Works of T.W. Lench & Company, situated in Yew Tree Lane, *c.* 1915. The façade remains very much the same today, and the spare ground on which the workmen are standing is presently the car park. (*Norah Smith*)

This formidable array of men are the St John Ambulance Brigade of Lenches, in the early 1920s. (*Ray Bridgewater*)

Whereas T.W. Lench made nuts and bolts, on the other side of Ross was the rivet works of Thomas Gadd, now demolished to make way for a small housing development. (*Ron Moss*)

Pictured in about 1940 in one of the works offices at T.W. Lench is James Harrold, an engineer by profession, who spent many years with the firm. Away from work, he was a prominent member of Providence Chapel. (*Margaret Sheward*)

During the First World War, in common with many other factories, T.W. Lench were contracted to provide munitions, and a group of women munitions workers pose for the camera watched by their male colleagues. (*Ray Parkes*)

The Doulton arm of the Dudley No. 2 Canal, mid-1950s. Clay was dug from Saltwells in Netherton and transported into the factory by barge, and finished materials were shipped out for distribution. The Sanitary Pottery Works quay was on the right-hand side, while rock from the Hailstone Quarry was moved from the left-hand side. (*BCLM*)

Three quarry men from the Hailstone Quarry, including in the centre James Rose, who was later unfortunately killed in an accident. (*Enid Hadley*)

A group of employees at the North Works of the Austin Motor Co. Ltd, 1918. It is evident from the large shell in the foreground that at that time they were employed in manufacturing munitions. Although the great majority of workers, especially women, were employed close to home, many from Rowley Regis and the surrounding districts of the Black Country travelled into Birmingham and the suburbs to assist in the war effort. Transport was provided either by rail or coach. (*Irene Pritchard*)

The pit-head at Rowley Hall Colliery, showing the horse-drawn carts waiting to be filled, early 1900s. (*CHAS*)

Coal trucks at Rowley Hall Colliery, *c*. 1900. Coal was loaded on to these trucks, which were operated via a rope-worked railway incline and delivered to the canal basin in Whiteheath. Note the moving cable and handbrakes on the wooden truck coming up to a junction in the tracks. (*CHAS*)

The mine-owner's car contrasts with the horse and wagon in this photograph of Oakham Pit No. 26, taken in 1928, just two years before it was closed. (*BCS*)

Another view of Bell End Colliery, with the filled coal tubs on the track, *c*. 1910. (*Ken Rock Collection*)

At the bottom of Powke Lane, on the opposite side to where the cemetery now stands, was Rowley Regis Gas Works and a small industrial development, seen here in about 1950. In the background the trees on the skyline border Lench's recreation ground and it is clear that the gas holder is still in use. (*Margaret Sheward*)

When he was the Duke of York, King George VI visited the factory of T.W. Lench and made such an impression on the workforce that at the time of his coronation in 1937 the whole factory was decorated with bunting and flags, as can be seen in this workshop. (*Author's Collection*)

Time for a short break for this group of Rowley quarry men as they pose for the camera in the early days of the twentieth century. (*BCLM*)

The Rowley Rag that was excavated from the quarries needed to be rendered into a size that was more easily workable, and here is the necessary equipment, which was simply called the 'Rowley Rag Crusher'. It was in use at Darby's Hill Quarry in 1907. (*Horace Wilson*)

A group of blacksmiths at Hailstone Quarry, with Ernest Dunn second from right, *c. 1920.* In addition to the many men who worked at the rock face, in order for the mines and quarries to function numerous other jobs had to be carried out. (*Kenneth Biggs*)

A Stokes & Downing lorry parked in the company yard, situated behind the endowed school premises, early 1950s. With the advent of motor vehicles, the smaller, usually single-person haulage businesses using horse and cart were inevitably phased out, and in Rowley village the lorries of Stokes & Downing became a common sight. (*David Eades*)

The parish church was not only a centre for raising spiritual concerns, but also provided leisure activities, and the Revd A. Dauglish is seen here with a team of gymnasts, thought to be outside the vicarage, *c.* 1914. (*Ray Parkes*)

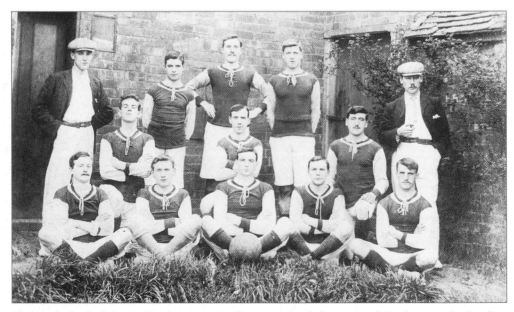

This early football team, Rowley Associated, were regarded as one of the best in the locality, although the details of this particular squad, photographed in the early twentieth century, are not known. (*Author's Collection*)

The Britannia Park Bowling Club, early 1960s. Back row (left to right): Ernie Dallow, Albert Kite, Billy Round, Ted Watton, Dick Harper, Ray Bridgewater, Gerry Evans, Bill Parsons, J. Hewitt; middle row: Henry Brettle, Reuben Ingram, Arthur Palmer; front row: Dennis Whittall, Albert Taylor, Joe Aldridge and Sammy Foster. (*Ray Bridgewater*)

The Rowley Village Cricket Club squad that beat the highly fancied Duport Sports to win the Don Kenyon Cricket competition, 21 August 1966. The club was formed from men returning from having done their National Service. Standing (left to right): Bert Thompson (President), Eric Wesson, Ken Hale, Roy Withers, Barry Parsons, Ken Kelmere, Tom Parry, Bill Sadler (Umpire), Steve Thompson (Scorer), Tony Holland; seated: Geoff Pestridge, Roy Pestridge, Stafford Screen, Dave Flavell and Doug Hale. (*Barry Parsons*)

Rowley Labour Club FC, 1952/3. This club played their matches at the bottom of Waterfall Lane, changing in the adjacent public house. Players seen here include: Tommy Hughes, Ray Devonport, Geoff Wood, Dan Shakespeare, Johnny Taylor and Ivan Yates. (*Dan Shakespeare*)

Rowley Labour Club FC a few years later, when they had now moved to play their home matches at the Bluebell Fields. Those identified include: Jimmy Devonport, Trevor Westwood, Trevor Taylor, Jim Adams, Alf Griffiths, Colin Smedley, Ken Dowell and Bert Cashmore. (*Trevor Westwood*)

A group of workers at the Britannia Works, Rowley village, early 1900s. The premises later became the home of the Endowed School Mission. (*George Smith*)

Enjoying himself on his bicycle among the Stokes & Downing lorries is Alan Skelton, 1960. Adjacent to the Britannia Works was this piece of ground, purchased by Mr Stokes and from where he eventually ran his haulage business. (*David Eades*)

In addition to playing football, the Park Rangers FC, who were based in Britannia Park, enjoyed many social functions, to which the whole family were invited. This happy group is enjoying one such outing, although the date and place are not remembered. (*Dennis Plant*)

The Excelsior Band of T.W. Lench were a popular and talented group of workers, who played at most of the major functions in the Blackheath and Rowley area and were particularly strong during the 1920s and 1930s when this was their line-up. (*Ray Parkes*)

Rescue team Number 2 at Knowle Colliery, one of the pits owned by H.S. Pitt & Company in the Rowley Regis and Dudley area, *c.* 1920. They are well equipped with breathing apparatus, the canary in its cage and a 'life-like' anatomical model. (*George Smith*)

HMS *Tumult* during the Second World War. In the war the residents of Rowley spent a lot of their leisure time raising funds and collecting items of comfort to send to members of the armed forces. The borough adopted HMS *Tumult* and, in order to maintain the Official Secrets Act, the captain wrote several anonymous letters of appreciation, particularly to the schoolchildren for their gifts of books which helped the seamen through the long hours at sea. (*Denise Macdonald*)

A group of employees take a break from their work at Steelace Manufacturing, Rowley village, 1940s. (*Vera Guest*)

An industrial unit in Portway Road, mid-1950s. In addition to quarrying the Rowley Rag, there was a growth in associated industries, such as the making of paving slabs and other concrete products, in the area around the quarries. (*Margaret Sheward*)

5

Shops
& Pubs

The Grange Inn during the severe winter of 1947. Occupying a prime position at the top of the village, diagonally opposite the parish church, this public house was formerly a private house, but was granted its licence when The Royal Oak in Blackheath town centre was demolished. (*Alice Perks*)

The step-father of the landlord standing outside the main entrance to The Ward Arms, situated right next to the gates of St Giles' Parish Church in Hawes Lane, *c.* 1950. Locals remember the pub being referred to by one of the vicars from the pulpit as 'The Well of Bethlehem' because several members of the congregation used to frequent the bar at the conclusion of the services. (*Jean Clift*)

For many years Mr Arthur Gilbert was the landlord of The Ward Arms, and he is seen here behind the bar, 11 April 1953. (*Jean Clift*)

George Aldridge, seen here in about 1925, ran a grocery shop from these premises in Rowley village, which had previously been a butcher's shop, from 1916. In 1921 he was appointed to be sub-post master, when the previous holder of that position retired, and he continued in that role for twenty-five years. The business carried on within the family for many years. The old post office was then replaced by a more modern building, and this remained in business until recent times, when the post office transferred to a modern convenience store. (*Mavis Bates*)

Seen in his Sunday best, Mr Lowe, the licensee of The Bull's Head for many years, takes his ease, *c.* 1920. The pub, at the junction of Hawes Lane and Tippetty Green, remained unchanged in external appearance until very recently, when it had a complete make-over and changed its name to The Chaplin. (*Marjorie Cashmore*)

Positioned in a convenient place for the thirsty quarry workers, The Portway Tavern in Tippetty Green is seen here in the late 1980s shortly before it was knocked down. The machinery on the left was part of Allsop's tar plant. (*David Westwood*)

The Royal Oak public house, Springfield, *c.* 1920. The landlord Joseph Plant is on the right and Tom Williams, who was the local representative of Ansells Brewery, on the left. (*Frank Taylor*)

For many years a local landmark, the post office at Springfield, 22 June 1969. Everyone called it Bayley's Post Office and it stood at the top of Springfield Lane at the junction with Dudley Road. (*CHAS*)

Another view of The Grange Inn, this time in better weather, mid-1950s. (*Derek Wroe*)

Ray Devonport (left) and Tom Wroe (right), father of the licensee, behind the bar at The Grange Inn, *c.* 1960. (*Derek Wroe*)

The Britannia Inn, which stands next to the park of the same name, underwent a complete renovation and face-lift in 1988, and here we can compare the pub before (in 1987, upper) and after (in 1989, lower) the work had taken place. In the top picture, the Co-op stores can be seen at the right of the shot. (*John Pardoe*)

Right at the top of the village was the shop belonging to the Tibbetts family, seen here in the early 1940s. Once inside it was a real 'Aladdin's Cave', with a wonderful range of goods kept stocked for such a small shop. To the left newspapers and sweets on display, but to the right was the barber and hairdressing side of the business. (*Enid Hadley*)

Three generations of the Tibbetts family are seen behind the shop counter in the mid-1950s (left to right): Gussey Male (daughter), Enid Male (granddaughter) and Gussey Tibbetts (mother). (*Malcolm Warby*)

To visit the Village Fish Shop, owned for many years by Dan Bennett, was a special treat, and generations have thrived on fish and chips in newspaper, dripping with salt and vinegar. If you wanted wet fish it meant a trip up the entry, to the rear of the premises. This photograph dates from about 1960 and the business is still conducted from this building today. (*Ray Parkes*)

William Mallin, born in 1864, and Betsy Tromans, born in 1865, photographed at the time of their betrothal. The originals are on large, hand-tinted lantern slides. William was born in Portway, where his father had a farm, and Betsy in Bell End, where her father was a grocer. William moved into the business on his marriage, and the shop became well known for the sale of home-made lemonade in bottles with large glass stoppers. The retail business was handed down through the next three generations. (*Anita Page*)

Mary Smith and a young helper outside Throne Stores shortly after the shop's opening. In 1920 William Skidmore and his family moved to Throne Farm, in Throne Road, from Smethwick, where they kept most farm animals, with the exception of sheep, and also grew vegetables and made their own butter. In the early 1930s he built this retail shop in Throne Road, and his daughter Mabel helped to run it from the age of fourteen. The building is now home to a dental practice. (*Mabel Smith*)

A group of ladies relax outside The Kings Arms public house in Rowley village, late 1940s. (*David Eades*)

6

People
& Events

A familiar sight to anyone visiting Britannia Park was Stan Slater, for many years a gardener, seen here tending the flowerbeds at the top end of the park, 1962. (*Mary Cutler*)

The officials of Rowley Regis Urban District Council, 1933. Back row (left to right): W.B. Eley (Rating Officer), F.T. Wilson (Secretary to Education Committee), J.T. Danks (Chief Finance Officer), A. Longfellow (Chief Sanitary Inspector); front row: Dr W.E. Roper-Saunders (Medical Officer of Health), C. Buckley (Clerk to the Council), L.J. Taylor (Surveyor). (*CHAS*)

Horace R. Wilson, son of the Secretary to Education Committee, became a teacher and worked in several schools in the borough. He is a well-known artist and local historian who has published several books, organises exhibitions and is in constant demand because of his widespread knowledge both of the immediate area and further afield. (*Horace Wilson*)

Sitting outside their cottage in Siviters
Lane are Mrs Williams and her daughters
Gwendoline Vera, Eugenia Mary and
Rachel at the end of the nineteenth
century. (*Anita Whitehouse*)

The family group photograph at the wedding of Tom Wallace and Emily Guest, taken in the front
garden of the bride's home in Rowley village, opposite The Britannia Inn, 1923. The cottages in the
right background of the picture, situated between the park and The Sir Robert Peel public house,
were known as Lillipot Row. (*Vera Guest*)

Edith Skelton among the outbuildings of The Swan public house in the village, 1946. At the time the property was owned by Mr Stokes. (*David Eades*)

Mr Joe Whittall was the caretaker at Siviters Lane school for twenty-two years, retiring from the position in 1971. At the annual speech day the headmistress Miss Westwood and the head girl presented him with gifts on behalf of the school. On the left is the chairman of the governors Councillor Mrs Evelyn Matthews. (*Maud Shaw*)

The last Mayor of the Borough Councillor Mrs Evelyn Matthews poses with the other elected members outside the Municipal Buildings in 1965. In 1966 Rowley Regis ceased to be an administrative area in its own right, when, together with the boroughs of Oldbury and Smethwick, local government reorganisation formed the County Borough of Warley. (*Author's Collection*)

Peter Archer, supported by his wife Miff, addressing a political rally in the early 1970s. Peter Kingsley Archer was born in 1926, and was elected as Member of Parliament for Rowley Regis & Tipton in the 1966 election, continuing to serve both that constituency and its replacement, Warley West, until 1992. He held many offices within Government, including Solicitor General from 1974 to 1979. A lawyer by profession, he was made QC in 1971 and became a member of the Privy Council in 1977. On retirement from the House of Commons, he joined the House of Lords, taking the title Baron Archer of Sandwell. The head of many voluntary organisations, Peter is a well-respected Methodist local preacher. (*Lord Archer*)

Some of the employees of the Rowley Regis Corporation made a visit to the Houses of Parliament, and are seen on the terrace with Arthur Henderson MP (later Lord Rowley), early 1960s. Among those present are Brian and Dora Bubb, Arthur Blakeway, Dennis Boxley, Sam Cope and Ada Taylor. (*Irene Harrold*)

Located on the Dudley Road, near to the Knowle Methodist Church, is the Springfield Working Men's Club, a popular meeting place for the area. Members were devastated when a fire gutted the building on 16 August 1990. (*Frank Taylor*)

James Woodhouse, painted by William Armfield Hobday at the age of eighty-one. Woodhouse was born in Rowley Regis in 1735, the son of a yeoman farmer. Having only the most basic schooling (leaving at age eight), he continued to be mainly self-educated, but was helped by the poet William Shenstone and other gentlemen patrons. He worked as a shoemaker, supplementing his income by teaching at the local endowed school, before being employed by Shenstone to help him lay out the grounds at the nearby Leasowes. He became a prolific writer of poetry, about which Dr Johnson wrote, 'He may make an excellent shoemaker, but can never make a great poet', however in later life he did modify this judgement. In 1766 he became land steward to Edward Montagu, husband of Elizabeth Montagu, one of the leading literary women of the eighteenth century. After a time he moved to London and kept a bookseller's shop near Grosvenor Square. He became well known in literary and society circles, but was killed when crossing the road in London in 1820. He was buried at St George's Chapel near Marble Arch. (*Horace Wilson*)

A charming group of bridesmaids posing outside St Giles' Parish Church, 1960s. In the background the grocery store of T.P. Moyle can be seen, with a 140 Midland Red bus going down the hill, and the blue police call-box on the corner. (*Enid Hadley*)

Some of the children from Rowley village gather outside the Steelace factory to celebrate the Coronation of Queen Elizabeth II, 1952. Among them are: Pamela Willetts, Jim Sidaway, Alan Grimshaw, Jill Aldridge, Pat Bennett, Fred Willetts, Vicky Barnbrook, Carol Bridgewater, Derek Aldridge, Stephen Payne, Roy Noott, Paul Bennett, Stephen Round and John Aldridge. (*Jill Rowe*)

The wedding of Ted Watton and Dora Aldridge, taken in the back garden of their home in Rowley village, with Siviters Lane in the background. The party comprises (left to right): Ethel Aldridge, George Aldridge, Dora Aldridge, Ted Watton, Howard Aldridge and Elsie Woodhall. (*Jill Rowe*)

Members of the congregation from St Giles' Parish Church before an outing to Blackpool, *c.* 1950. The group includes: Dave Mulcaster, Margaret Humphries, Mavis Aldridge and Alice Griffiths. (*Mavis Bates*)

Scouting has been a popular activity in the village and the Cub and Scout troop are seen here outside their headquarters in Hawes Lane, *c.* 1954. Mr Biggs was Scoutmaster for many years, and is on the far left of this picture. (*Paul Harris*)

Elizabeth Gussey Rose Tibbetts is seen in the garden of her house in Currall Road, looking towards the church, 1970s. In addition to the hours she spent running the hairdressing and newsagent's shop (*see* p. 100), she still found time to look after chickens and turkeys. (*Enid Hadley*)

The employees of Rowley Regis Council, outside the Municipal Buildings, 1953. (*Nellie Holloway*)

A party of the gay young things of the area pictured in Lenches Park, 1925. Among the group are: Daisy Harrold, Jack Homer and Irene Harrold. (*Irene Harrold*)

A regular summer and autumn feature for many Rowley families was the annual working holiday to the hop fields of Worcestershire and Herefordshire. All members of the family became involved in the labour intensive activity, many taking most, if not all, of their worldly goods with them. As part of his evangelical mission, described earlier (*see* p. 50), George Aldridge was a regular visitor to the workers, and we see him here on the left of this group. (*Jill Rowe*)

The Rowley Angling Society had fishing grounds in Coalport, Shropshire, and once a year held a Chairman/Secretary fishing match, and some of the participants in the 1955 competition are seen here. The men are: Billy Mainwaring, Oliver Hindmarsh, Norman Hindmarsh, Arthur Brookes, Ray Poole, Jim Sidaway, Jack Willetts, Arthur Salisbury, Ray Bridgewater, Howard Aldridge, C. Weston, Sam Rudge and Cliff Harris. (*Jill Rowe*)

In 1920 Lizzie Pardoe got married and held the celebrations at Portway Hall, where she had been born twenty years earlier. Her father Mr David Pardoe had purchased the Hall, seen in the background, and its 250-acre estate a few years before his daughter's birth. The well-dressed guests are clearly relishing the occasion. (*Trevor Westwood*)

Members of the Air Raid Precautions (ARP) meet at the wedding reception of one of their members, Edna Parsons, in 1940 or 1941. Edna's parents kept a sweet shop in Carnegie Road. Edna and her husband Wilf emigrated to Canada at the end of the Second World War. In addition to the bride, the ladies are: Elizabeth Neil, Agnes Bagley, G. Hardgest, Ann Homer, J. Johnson, L. Taylor, Joan Cox, Elizabeth Ashman, Annie Southall, Joan Dingley, M. Bennett, Annie Downing, Annie Barrett, Irene Pritchard, Rose Wilkens, G. Lowe, Mabel Hooper. The other man is Howard Lowe. (*Irene Pritchard*)

Cecil Westwood and Louie Chandler were married at 8.00 a.m. on 5 August 1933 at Oldbury Wesley Chapel. The bride's family owned the still-working Lion Farm in Throne Road, and the groom was one of the brothers of Albert Westwood, Mayor of Rowley Regis. Cecil was for many years a Methodist local preacher and also served as Verger of St Giles' Parish Church. (*Trevor Westwood*)

Sir John Frederick Bridge, known as Sir Frederick, was born in Oldbury on 5 December 1844. He spent much of his childhood with his mother's relatives, John and Mallin, at Portway Farm. At the age of six he was admitted to Rochester Cathedral School, where he remained until 1859. Following a variety of posts he was appointed organist at Holy Trinity Church, Windsor, then at Manchester Cathedral until 1875, when he was appointed as organist and choirmaster at Westminster Abbey. He was conductor of the Royal Choral Society from 1896 until 1922, and was knighted in 1897. He died in the cloisters of Westminster Abbey on 18 March 1924. He was known by the nickname of 'Westminster Bridge' to distinguish him from his brother, organist at Chester Cathedral and known as 'Chester Bridge'. (*Author's Collection*)

Sir Frederick Bridge opens a garden party in Lenches Park to raise money to complete the purchase of bells and to clear the debt for the newly built St Giles' Parish Church on 23 June 1923. He wrote to the vicar expressing his delight at being asked to carry out this task, saying that he had fond memories of the old church and his time at the old farm. (*Author's Collection*)

The new crematorium at Rowley Regis cemetery was dedicated in the mid-1960s. In the upper photograph Councillor Mrs Evelyn Matthews is seen talking to the Town Clerk, while the choir of St Giles' Parish Church is assembled on the left, including Jack and Edith Edgington, Alan Roberts, Geoff Robertson, Ian Harrold, Jack and Mrs Brown and Mrs Davenport. The clergy include the Revd S.B. Coley, the Revd W.W. Ion and Revd T.L. Haywood. In the lower picture Mrs Matthews is greeting the Rt Revd L. Wilson (Bishop of Birmingham), with the Revd J. Farmer and the Mayor of Rowley Regis Councillor Vic Wakeman on the left. (*Malcolm Warby*)

The amusement area in Britannia Park has provided countless children with pleasure over the years, and here we see the James twins enjoying a spin on the roundabout, with the swings and The Britannia Inn in the background, 1960s. (*Vera Guest*)

The local authority provided allotments for those interested in furthering their gardening skills, situated off Siviters Lane at the top end of Britannia Park. One of the most prolific prize-winners in the council-run competitions over the years was Ray Bridgewater, seen here surrounded by his cabbage plants in the 1970s. (*Ray Bridgewater*)

Born at Rowley Hall on 29 October 1888, the eldest son of Frederick and Elizabeth North, Frederick William Severne North achieved international fame as the stage designer Paul Shelving. His sets and costumes for most of the major theatre producers in the land, especially Sir Barry Jackson at the Birmingham Repertory Theatre, brought him awards and acclaim. He is seen here at work on one of his mock-ups. He died at Warwick Hospital on 5 June 1968 and is buried at Leamington Cemetery. (*Photograph by kind permission of Sir Barry Jackson Trust and Birmingham City Council, Department of Leisure and Culture, Libraries Division*)

Mr Chandler, father of Louie (see p. 115), kept the large Lion Farm in Throne Road, and he is seen here with a selection of his livestock, 1920s. (*Trevor Westwood*)

With their polished helmets and interesting selection of apparatus, the Rowley Regis Fire Brigade of 1901/2 poses in front of Trinity School. The fireman standing behind appliance no. 3 was Benjamin Price, who lived in a cottage next door to Britannia Park, and was one of the first to spot the fire at St Giles' Parish Church in 1913. It is believed that the gentleman in the top hat at the left of the picture is one of the influential Bassano family members. (*Margaret Green*)

Almost forty years later, in 1939, the brass helmets have given way to flat hats and the engines have been modernised, but the firemen's evident pride in their work is undiminished. (*CHAS*)

The body of men who made up the Britannia Park Sons of Rest pose in front of the pavilion in the park, which they used as their headquarters until the current purpose-built hall was constructed, *c.* 1938. The gentleman on the extreme right of the back row, wearing his official hat, is Jack Hollick, the park keeper, and to his right, in Salvation Army uniform, is Tom Siviter. Ben Price is on the front row. (*Margaret Green*)

The annual presentation evening for prize-winners of the Rowley Regis and District Angling Society, *c.* 1960. Left to right: Lord Forrester (of Willey Hall, who owned the rights of the club's fishing ground on the River Severn between Coalport and Linley), Mrs Spring, Councillor Albert Spring (Mayor of Halesowen and member of club), Cyril Law, Len Bagley, Dennis Taylor, Arthur Salisbury (Chairman) and Howard Aldridge (Secretary). (*Mavis Bates*)

The residents of Park Avenue celebrate the Queen's Silver Jubilee with a street party held on 7 June 1977. (*CHAS*)

Ray Bridgewater is being presented with the winner's cup in the first allotment competition organised by Sandwell Metropolitan Borough Council following local government reorganisation in 1974. Left to right: Donald McGibbon (Parks and Amenities Department), Councillor Bill Walker (Mayor of Sandwell), Georgina Everitt (Local Authority Press Secretary) and Ray Bridgewater. (County Express)

Numerous happy hours have been spent in small aluminium paddleboats, and here Jean Grove, Marion and Jean Davies, all of Bell End, enjoy the experience, *c.* 1940. To many Rowley children the massive expanse of water (or so it seemed) that was the paddling and boating pool in Britannia Park offered an adventure. The park keeper's house is in the background. (*Jean Bubb*)

The last family to occupy Rowley Hall were the Nootts, who are seen here in the grounds of the Hall, *c.* 1910. Standing (left to right): Alfred Stanley, Sidney, Edward William, Alfred Hickman, Ada Lilian and Arthur Harry; seated, middle row: Sarah Ellen, Maude Evelyn, Sarah Annie and George Frederick Llewellyn; seated, at front: Nora Hellena and John Herbert. Inserted in the cameo at the back is Gwendolyn, who had emigrated to the USA. (*Marjorie Cashmore*)

The Taylor family outside their cottage at 123 Rowley village, which was situated roughly where the top of Britannia Road is now, *c.* 1905. Standing (left to right): Joe Taylor, David Taylor, Absolom Taylor, James Taylor, George Taylor and Tom Taylor; seated: Elizabeth Taylor, Anne Taylor (née White) and Selina Taylor. (*Mary Cutler*)

Anne Taylor at the cottage door with her son David Taylor, *c.* 1905. David is saying his final goodbyes, as he is about to leave for the USA. This was the last time he was to see his mother and it must have been an emotive moment, captured for posterity by the camera. (*Mary Cutler*)

William Tobias Harrold and Mary Ann
Ruston were both born in 1858 and
married in 1878. They lived in various
parts of Rowley and William worked at
the collieries as a stationary engine driver.
In this photograph six of their seven
children are featured, left to right: Polly
(born 1885), Millie (1892), Lily (1879),
Will (1890), Lois (1880) and Albert
(1883). (*Gwen Sewell*)

Albert Harrold followed the call to arms and
joined the Oxford & Bucks Light Infantry
during the First World War. At this time he was
a married man with four children under the age
of six. He never returned from the war, being
killed in action on 25 September 1915, and is
remembered at the memorial at Ypres. His widow
Sarah was well known in the village as she kept the
general stores in Bell End, for many years working with
her son Fred and later her daughter Rene. (*Author's
Collection*)

A final reminder that most of Rowley's fame and fortune has revolved around the natural resources of Rowley Rag, and this picture is dedicated to those many people who through the years have lost their lives or have suffered terrible injuries in excavating the stone, without which our road system would not have been able to develop. (*Author's Collection*)

With the advent of more mechanical methods of laying the roads, the quarries formed subsidiary companies, one of which was Van de Travers, and Frank Taylor, Zach Spittle and Bill Ettle are here seen taking a break from the use of the road roller, 1950s. These men are the descendants of those described in the poem on the opposite page. (*Frank Taylor*)

Rowley Roadmen by Geoffrey Bubb

I saw roadmen out repairing Rowley roads.
Eight or ten of them.
Young, massive men,
Flesh dark from sun and dirt,
Huge chests covered by scant T-shirt.
Hair blond bleached by ultra-violet light.
Skin, across mighty muscle, tight.
Mountain men with glistening flesh;
Tree-trunk arms and tattooed chest.
Heads held high
Against the azure sky,
Like Eastwood cowboys –
'Into town they strode'–
These artisans were on the Rowley Road.

Amid a scent from shimmering pitch
They set to work about a sunken ditch.
Goliaths, untroubled by
Backbreaking, bending
And toil never ending.
Earshattering sound –
A ceaseless cacophony all around
As hammers throb and jerk
In vicelike grips.
The roadway opens; rips
Beneath their feet –
The road, all squared off; geometric neat.

Grumbling rollers slowly
Smooth the tar.
Size nine shovels collect
Escaping, errant, inky 'stars'.
At last, the throbbing died.
Slowly the roadmen walk away.
Like strange industrial walking sticks
Shovels sounded, click, click, clicks;
A secret message which,
To those who know the roadman code
Said, 'So ends another working day.'

Geoff Bubb, who after taking early retirement took up the pen, is a prolific writer and his name is seldom missing from the correspondence columns of newspapers as diverse as the *Express* and *Star* and *The Times* and *Daily Telegraph*. He also contributes on a regular basis to the *Black Country Bugle* and the *Blackcountryman*, and this poem was published in October 2000. It is reproduced with grateful thanks.

ACKNOWLEDGEMENTS

Thanks are expressed to all those individuals and organisations that have loaned pictures for this publication, and these have been credited to the original photographer wherever possible, and failing that to the person loaning the image. Permission to use copyright photographs has been sought where this has been known, and apologies are extended for inadvertent use of any material.

Special thanks must be extended to Jeff Jephcott, editor (News Group), for the use of photographs and material from the *County Express*; the Black Country Living Museum (BCLM); the Black Country Society (BCS); the *Black Country Bugle*, and Sandwell Community History and Archive Service (CHAS); and individually to Ken Rock, Malcolm Warby, Maud Shaw and Horace Wilson.

The author intends to donate his profits to the funds of St Giles' Parish Church and Blackheath Central Methodist Church, and thanks all who will contribute to these appeals by purchasing this publication.

A group of Black Country miners in the early 1900s. (*Ken Rock Collection*)